My first book o

·····································

PORTUGUESE

·····································

words

Food

corn
o milho

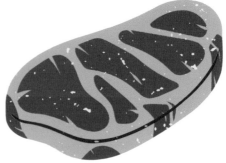

meat
a carne

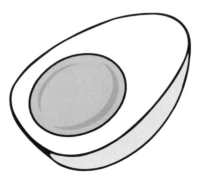

egg
o ovo

tomato
o tomate

pasta
a massa

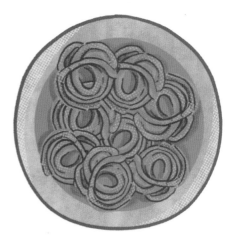

Comida

milk
o leite

pizza
a pizza

bread
o pão

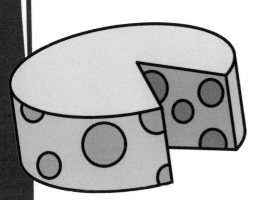

salmon
o salmão

cheese
o queijo

Garden

watering can
o regador

bucket
o balde

rake
o ancinho

leaf
a folha

flower
a flor

wheelbarrow
os carrinho de mão

Jardim

ladybug
a joaninha

soil
o solo

sunflower
o girassol

grasshopper
o gafanhoto

fence
a cerca

earthworm
a minhoca

Clothes

t-shirt
a camiseta

shoes
os sapatos

winter hat
o gorro

trousers
as calças

dress
o vestido

Roupa

shorts
o short

belt
o cinto

jacket
a jaqueta

socks
os meias

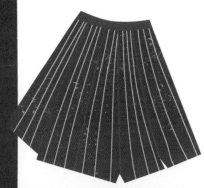

skirt
a saia

Room

clock
o relógio

painting
a pintura

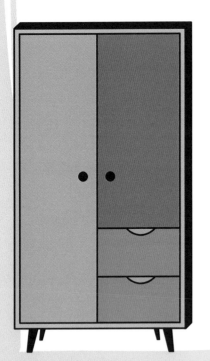

lamp
a lâmpada

armchair
a poltrona

wardrobe
o guarda roupa

Quarto

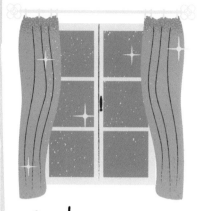

window
a janela

light
a luz

plant
a planta

sofa
as sofá

bed
a cama

rug
o tapete

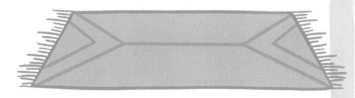

Farm animals

sheep
a ovelha

cow
a vaca

chick
o pintinho

duck
o pato

pig
o porco

Animais da fazenda

bee
a abelha

dog
o cachorro

hen
a galinha

bull
o tuoro

rabbit
o coelho

Forest

bird
o pássaro

trunk
o tronco

deer
o veado

tree
a árvore

hedgehog
o ouriço

pine cone
a pinha

Floresta

mushroom
o cogumelo

rowan
a sorva

fox
a raposa

bear
o urso

boar
o javali

squirrel
o esquilo

Street

bicycle
a bicicleta

car
o carro

road sign
a placa de trânsito

house
a casa

pedestrian
o pedestre

traffic lights
o sinal de trânsito

Rua

buildings
edifícios

bench
o banco

trash can
o cesto
de lixo

bus
os ônibus

street
a rua

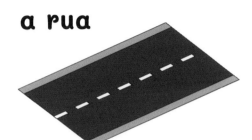

lorry
o caminhão

street lamp
a âmpada
de rua

People

father
o pai

mother
a mãe

angler
o pescador

neighbor
a vizinha

boy
o menino

cook
o cozinheir

girl
a menina

Gente

policeman
o policial

doctor
o médico

painter
o pintora

astronaut
astronauta

friends
amigos

elders
anciãos

guitarist
guitarrista

school

school supplies
material escolar

breakfast
o café da manhã

teacher
o professor

scissors
a tesoura

crayon
o creiom

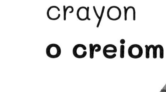

backpack
a mochila

Escola

blackboard
a lousa

medal
a medalha

pencil
o lápis

children
crianças

globe
o globo

book
o livro

shapes

square
o quadrado

circle
o círculo

triangle
o triângulo

heart
o coração

star
a estrela

Formas

arrow
a seta

crescent
o crescente

rectangle
o retângulo

diamond
o diamante

pentagon
o pentágono

Wild animals

giraffe
a girafa

monkey
o macaco

toucan
o tucano

zebra
a zebra

elephant
o elefante

Animais selvagens

tiger
o tigre

panda
o panda

snake
a serpente

hippopotamus
o hipopótamo

crocodile
o crocodilo

Kitchen

bowl
a tigela

flour
a farinha

kettle
a chaleira

mixer
a batedeira

grater
o ralador

cutlery
os talheres

Cozinha

sugar
o açúcar

toaster
a torradeira

fridge
o frigorífico

microwave
o microonda

oven
o forno

ingredients
ingredientes

Numbers

1

one
um/uma

2

two
dois/duas

3

three
três

four
quatro

4

five
cinco

5

Números

6 six **seis**

7 seven **sete**

eight **oito** **8**

9 nine **nove**

ten **dez** **10**

Printed in Great Britain
by Amazon